Facts About the Millipede

By Lisa Strattin

© 2022 Lisa Strattin

FREE BOOK

FREE FOR ALL SUBSCRIBERS

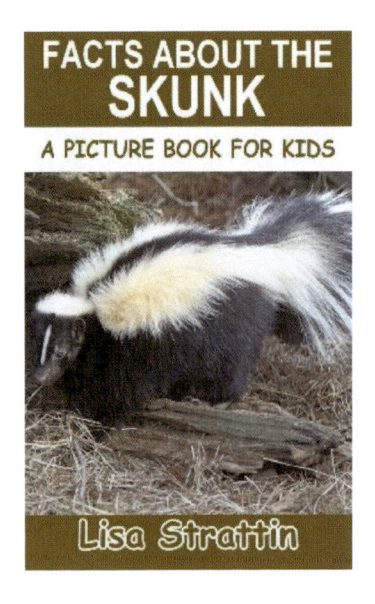

LisaStrattin.com/Subscribe-Here

BOX SET

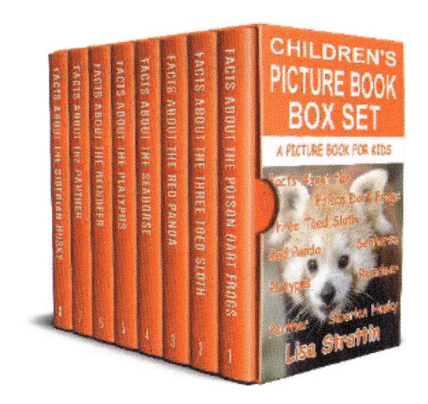

- **FACTS ABOUT THE POISON DART FROGS**
- **FACTS ABOUT THE THREE TOED SLOTH**
  - **FACTS ABOUT THE RED PANDA**
  - **FACTS ABOUT THE SEAHORSE**
  - **FACTS ABOUT THE PLATYPUS**
  - **FACTS ABOUT THE REINDEER**
  - **FACTS ABOUT THE PANTHER**
- **FACTS ABOUT THE SIBERIAN HUSKY**

LisaStrattin.com/BookBundle

Facts for Kids Picture Books by Lisa Strattin

Little Blue Penguin, Vol 92

Chipmunk, Vol 5

Frilled Lizard, Vol 39

Blue and Gold Macaw, Vol 13

Poison Dart Frogs, Vol 50

Blue Tarantula, Vol 115

African Elephants, Vol 8

Amur Leopard, Vol 89

Sabre Tooth Tiger, Vol 167

Baboon, Vol 174

Sign Up for New Release Emails Here

LisaStrattin.com/subscribe-here

All rights reserved. No part of this book may be reproduced by any means whatsoever without the written permission from the author, except brief portions quoted for purpose of review.

All information in this book has been carefully researched and checked for factual accuracy. However, the author and publisher makes no warranty, express or implied, that the information contained herein is appropriate for every individual, situation or purpose and assume no responsibility for errors or omissions. The reader assumes the risk and full responsibility for all actions, and the author will not be held responsible for any loss or damage, whether consequential, incidental, special or otherwise, that may result from the information presented in this book.

All images are free for use or purchased from stock photo sites or royalty free for commercial use.

Some coloring pages might be of the general species due to lack of available images.

I have relied on my own observations as well as many different sources for this book and I have done my best to check facts and give credit where it is due. In the event that any material is used without proper permission, please contact me so that the oversight can be corrected.

COVER IMAGE

https://www.flickr.com/photos/blairgannon/7756681666/

ADDITIONAL IMAGES

https://www.flickr.com/photos/berniedup/9598625908/

https://www.flickr.com/photos/yimhafiz/2516700912/

https://www.flickr.com/photos/aidan_jones/1236252050/

https://www.flickr.com/photos/goosmurf/5962744571/

https://www.flickr.com/photos/mikeprince/50935116782/

https://www.flickr.com/photos/43555660@N00/16073527487/

https://www.flickr.com/photos/68177867@N00/305006731/

https://www.flickr.com/photos/m-a-r-t-i-n/23106564491/

https://www.flickr.com/photos/davidden/2210327776/

https://www.flickr.com/photos/gails_pictures/39693300824/

Contents

INTRODUCTION 9
CHARACTERISTICS 11
APPEARANCE 13
LIFE STAGES 15
LIFE SPAN 17
SIZE 19
HABITAT 21
DIET 23
FRIENDS AND ENEMIES 25
SUITABILITY AS PETS 27

INTRODUCTION

Millipedes are long, thin creatures that are often mistaken for centipedes. They vary in color, but are usually brown or black, and can reach up to four inches in length. Millipedes have two pairs of legs (sometimes four) on each segment of their bodies, while centipedes have only one pair. Millipedes are not harmful to humans, but they can be a nuisance if they find their way into your home. They are often found in moist areas, such as gardens or basements. If you find a millipede in your home, the best way to get rid of it is to simply sweep it up and release it outside.

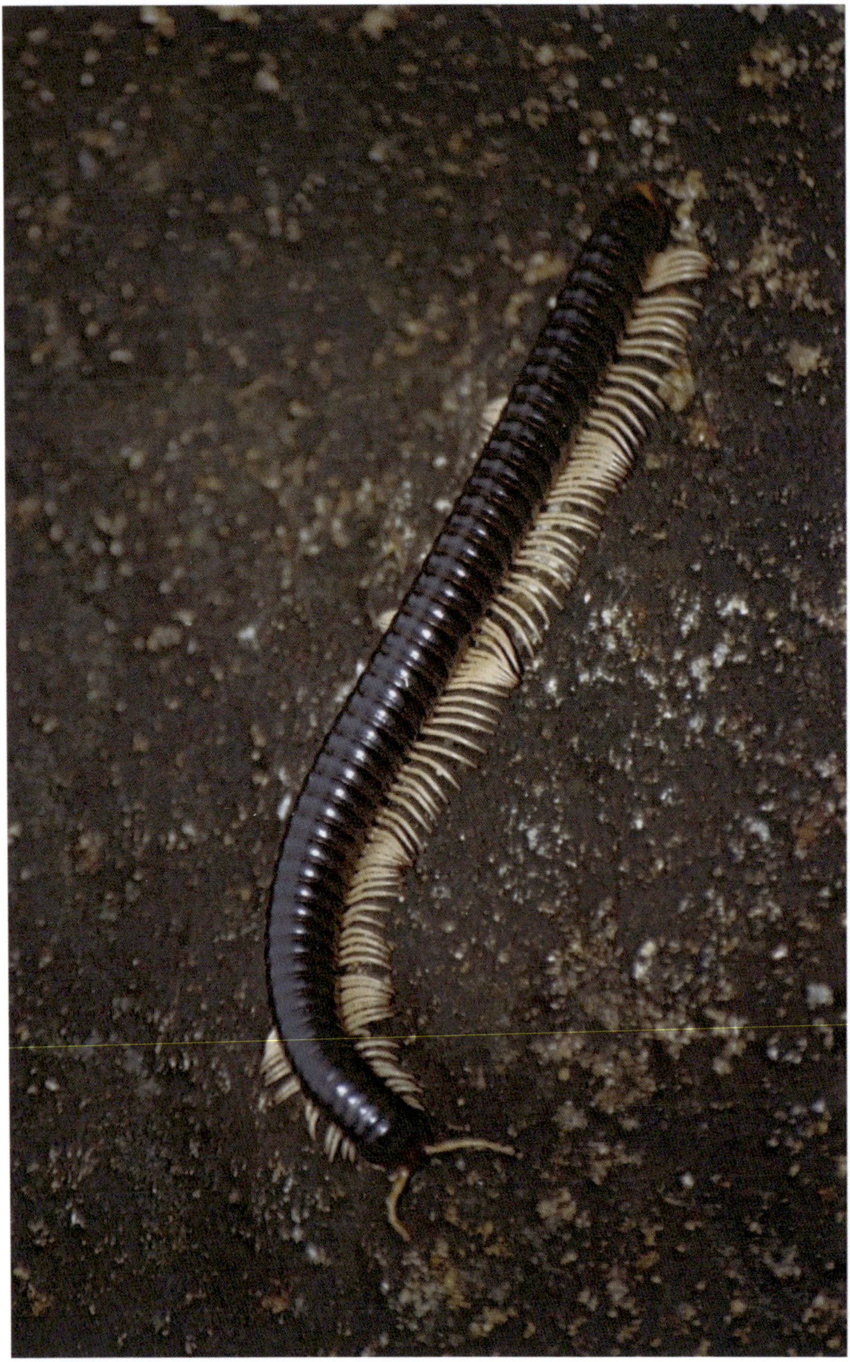

CHARACTERISTICS

Millipedes are small, soil-dwelling animals that are known for their long, segmented bodies. Most species of millipede have two pairs of legs per segment, but some millipedes can have up to four pairs. The number of legs a millipede has depends on the species; some millipedes can have as few as 10 legs, while others can have up to 750.

They are not fast bugs; they move slowly and deliberately, often using their legs to feel their way forward in the dark. Millipedes also have a pair of spiracles, or openings, on each side of their body that they use to breathe. Millipedes are nocturnal animals that spend the day hiding in dark places such as under rocks or in leaf litter.

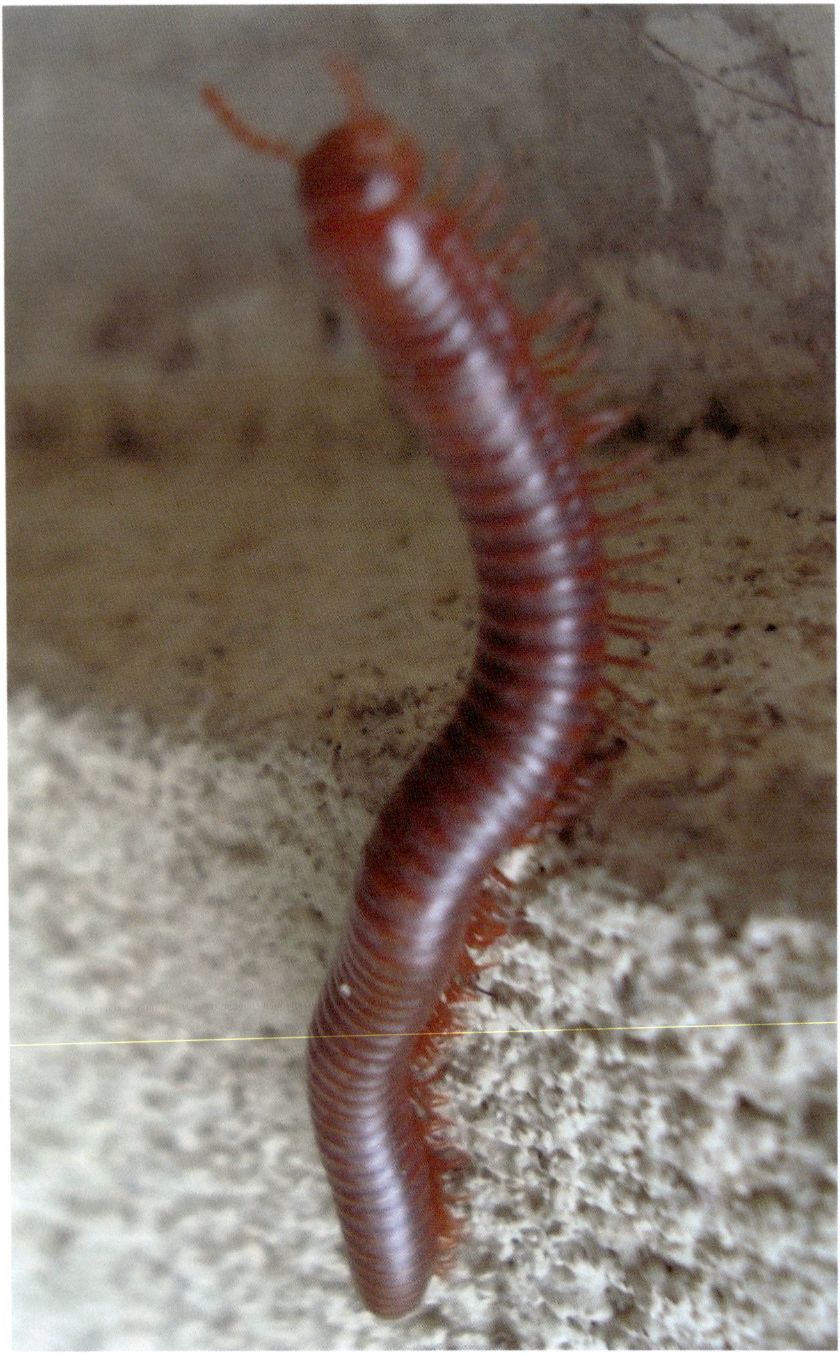

APPEARANCE

Most Millipedes have elongated cylindrical bodies, although some species are flattened torso-ventrally. The legs are perpendicular to the body, giving millipedes rippling locomotion. The number of legs varies among species but is typically in the range of 30-90 pairs.

A pair of antennae is at the front end of the body, and behind these are a set of mouthparts used for chewing. Most millipedes are herbivorous, feeding on dead leaves and other organic matter. Some species scavenge for animal carcasses, while others are predators of small animals such as insects.

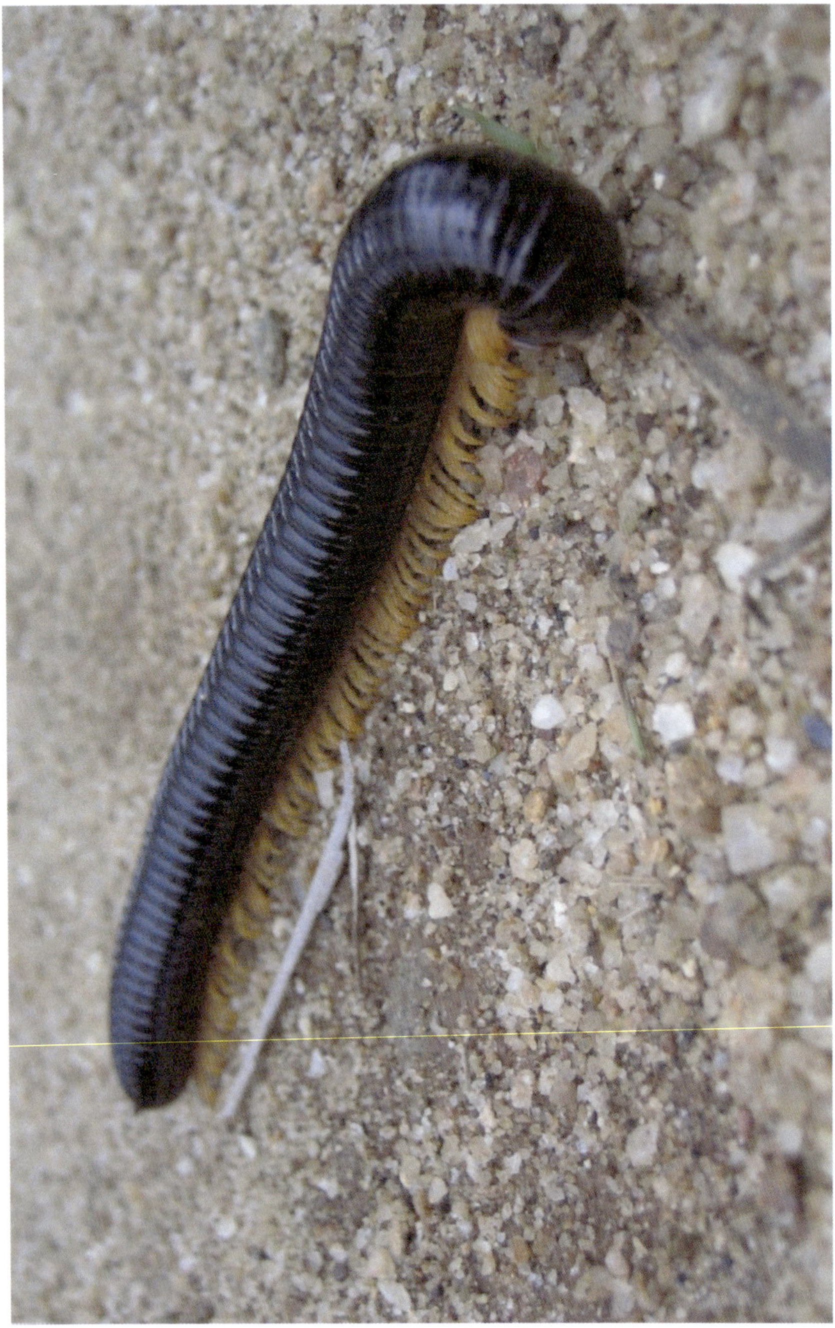

LIFE STAGES

Millipedes go through four main life stages – egg, larva, pupa, and adult-

Egg

The first stage, egg, lasts anywhere from 2 weeks to 6 months depending on the species. During this stage, Millipede eggs are often laid in moist soil or rotting vegetation.

Larva

Once they hatch, the larvae resemble small adults. They typically have fewer body segments and shorter legs than adults, but they otherwise look very similar.

Pupa

The pupa stage is a brief transitional phase between larva and adult. During this stage, Millipede larvae spin silken cocoons around themselves and undergo metamorphosis.

Adult

Once they emerge from their cocoons, Millipedes are fully-grown adults.

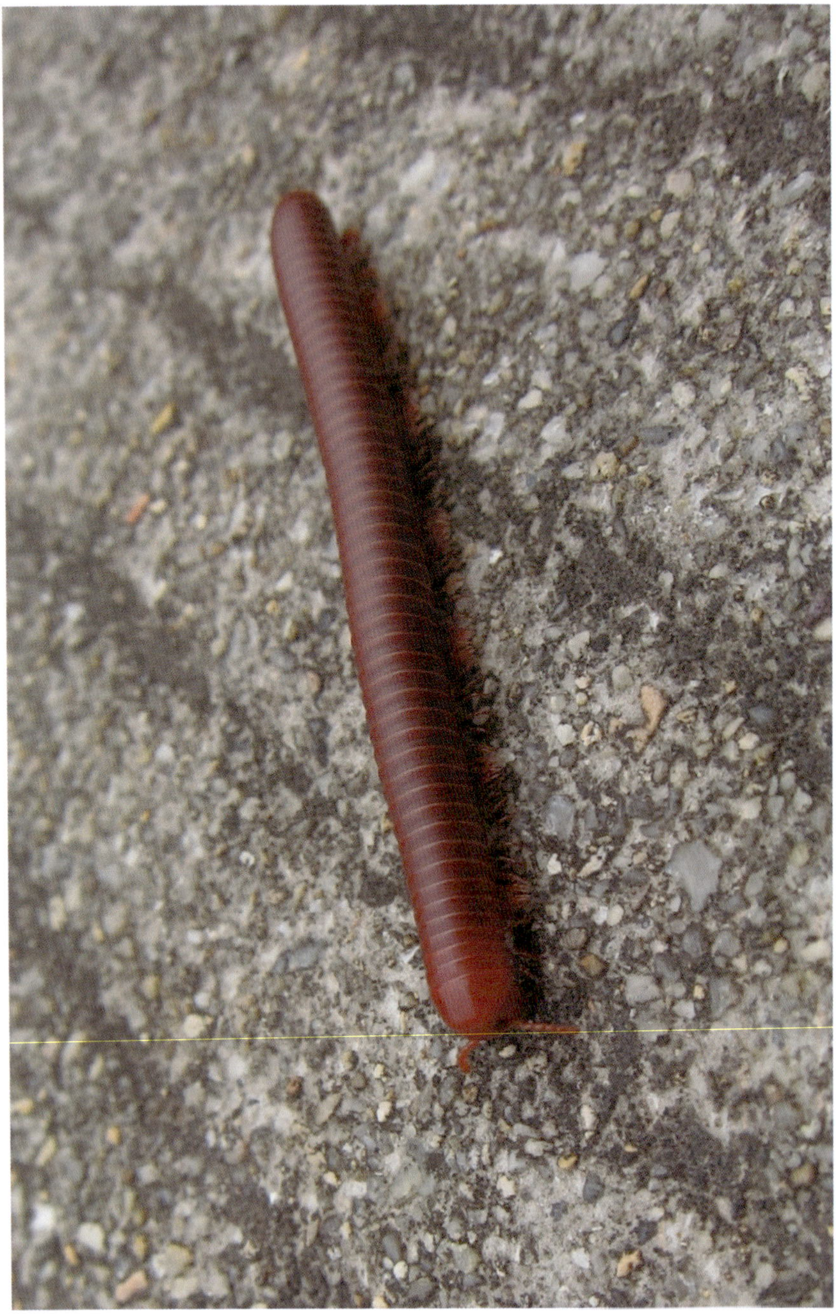

LIFE SPAN

Most Millipedes live 2-5 years, although there are some species with lifespans exceeding 10 years.

The world's longest recorded lifespan for a Millipede belongs to the species *Illacme plenipes*, which can live up to 30 years in captivity!

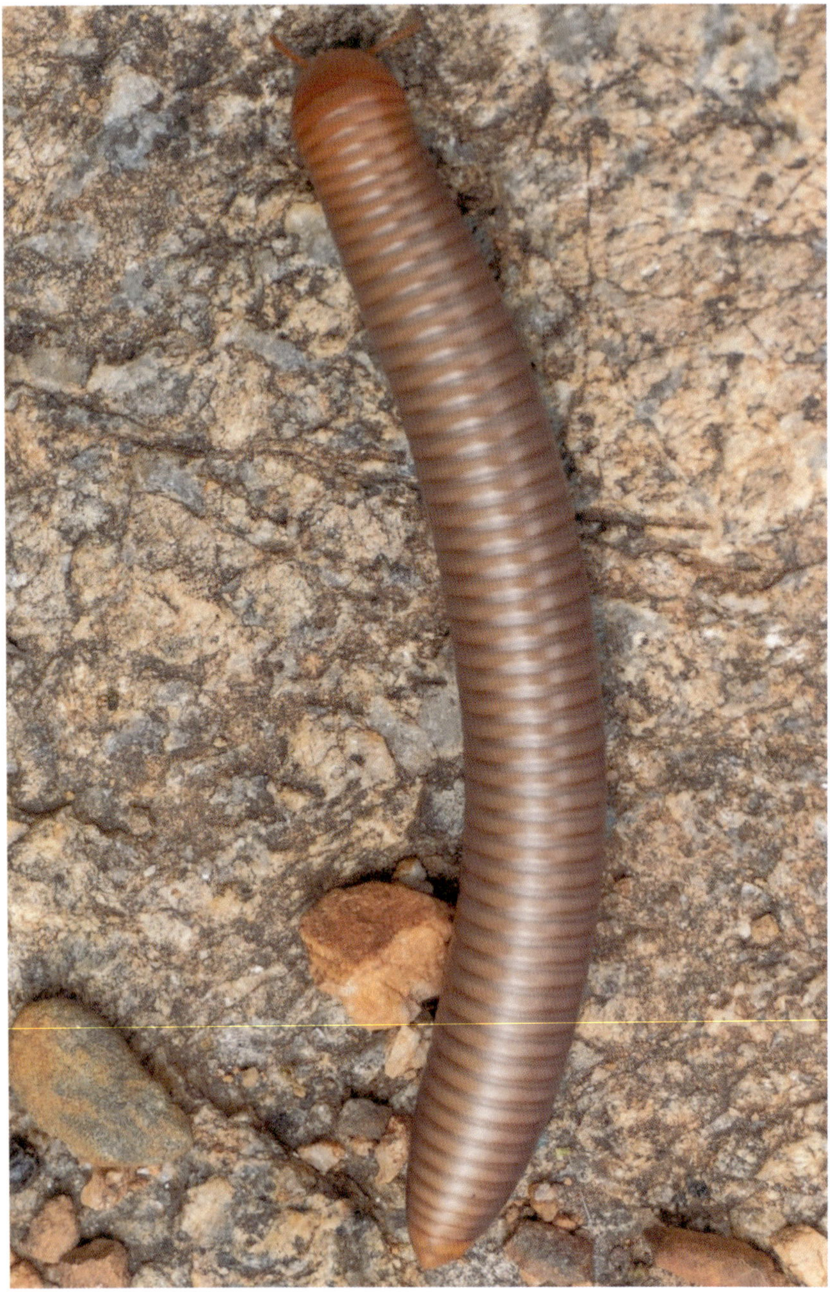

SIZE

Millipedes come in a wide variety of sizes, from the very small to the quite large. The smallest Millipedes are just a few millimeters long, while the largest can be over 11 inches in length. There is a great deal of variation in size even within a single species. For example, the common Millipede can range in size from 2 to 3 inches. However, most fall somewhere in the middle range, with adults measuring 4 to 6inches in length.

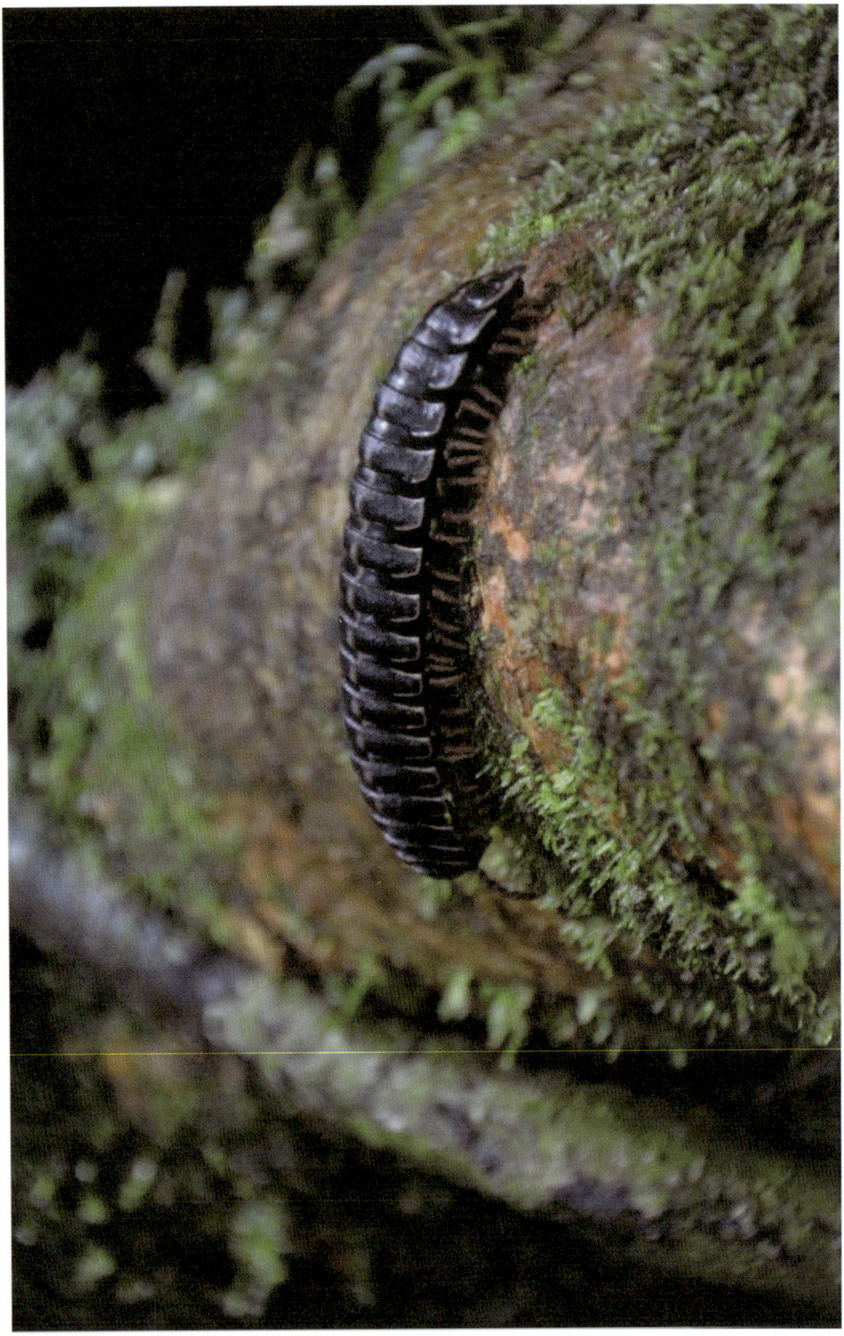

HABITAT

Millipedes are found in a wide variety of habitats all around the world. They are most commonly found in moist, shady areas such as forests, gardens, and lawns. Millipedes also live in caves, deserts, and even underwater. In fact, one species of millipede is known to live at the bottom of the ocean!

While most millipedes are happy to live on the ground, some species live in trees or underground. No matter where they live, all need a damp environment in order to survive. Without moisture, Millipedes will quickly dry out and die. For this reason, Millipedes are often observed after rainfall or during periods of high humidity.

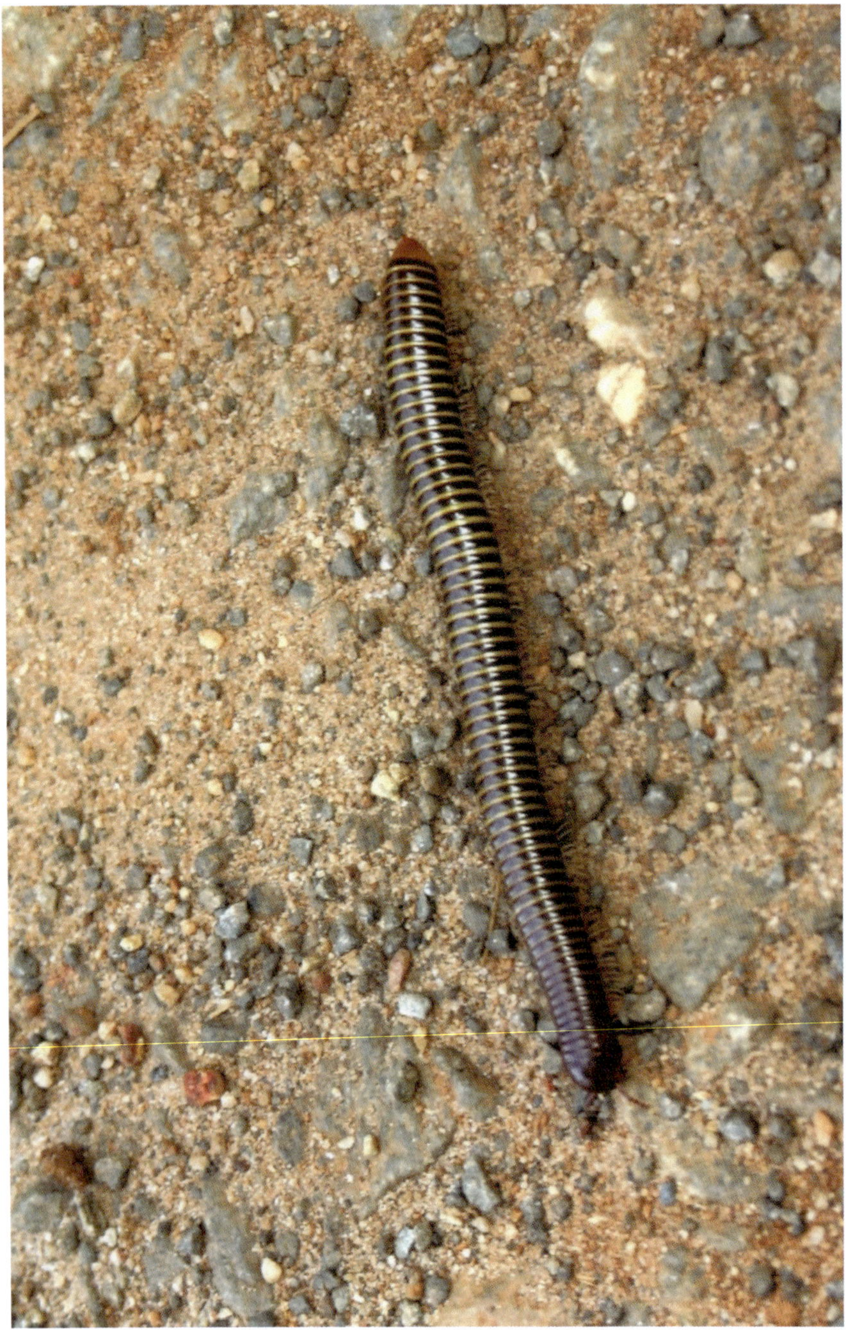

DIET

Millipedes are mostly vegetarian. Their diet consists of dead leaves, wood, and other plant matter. While millipedes will occasionally eat small insects, they mainly rely on plants for sustenance. In addition to their vegetarian diet, they also have a very slow metabolism. This is likely due to the low nutritional content of their food. As a result, Millipedes can live for long periods of time without eating anything at all!

They play an important role in the decomposition process, and their ability to convert dead leaves into nutrients helps to keep forests healthy. Without Millipedes, the ground would be covered in a thick layer of rotting vegetation, which would provide a perfect breeding ground for disease-carrying pests.

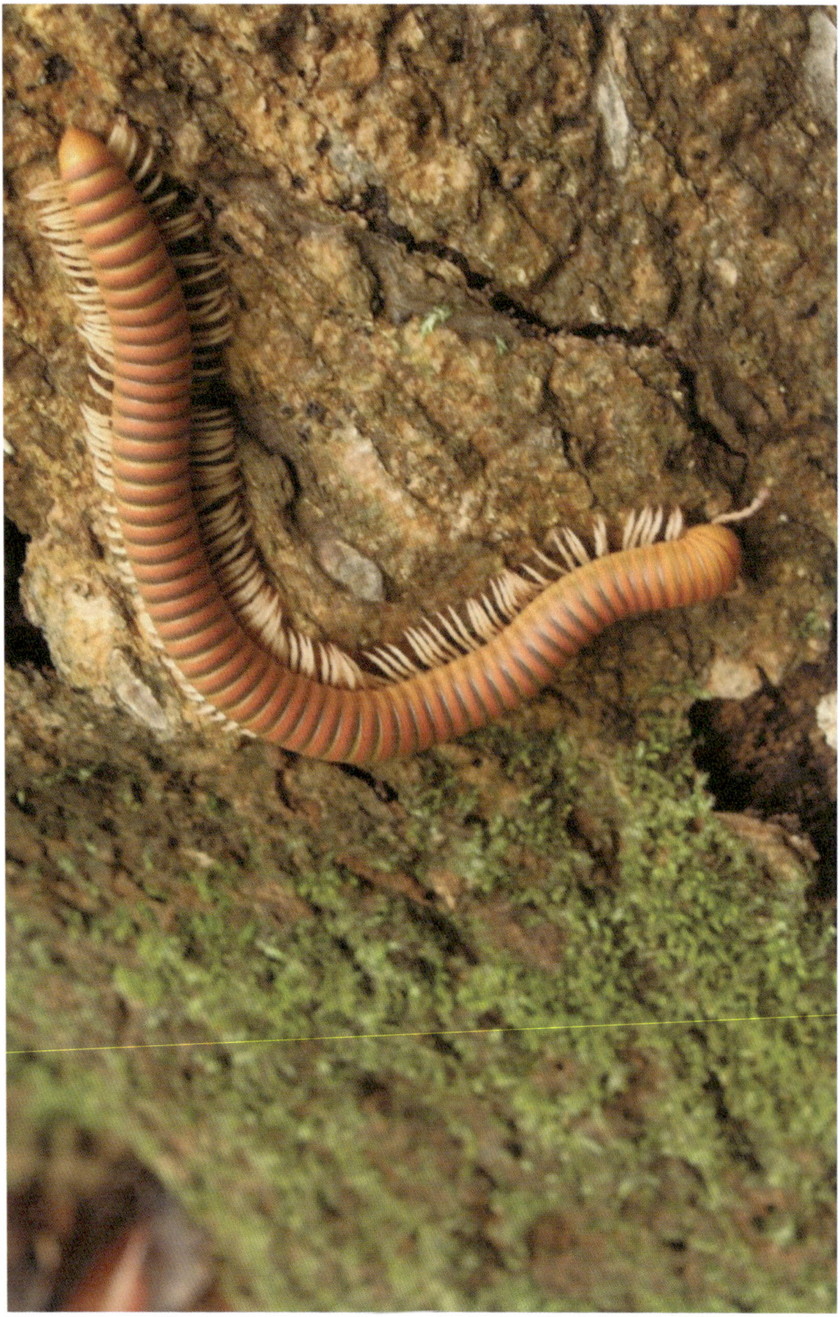

FRIENDS AND ENEMIES

Millipedes are mostly solitary creatures, but they will congregate in large numbers when conditions are favorable. For example, during periods of drought, they will often migrate en masse in search of more humid environments.

Some species of Millipede will form friendships with other animals, such as frogs, lizards, and snakes. In fact, these relationships can be beneficial for both parties; the Millipede provides the reptile with a ready source of food while the reptile offers the Millipede protection from predators.

There are a few enemies that pose a threat to these creatures. Chief among these are centipedes, which are known to prey on them. In addition, some species of spiders, birds, and mammals will also eat Millipedes.

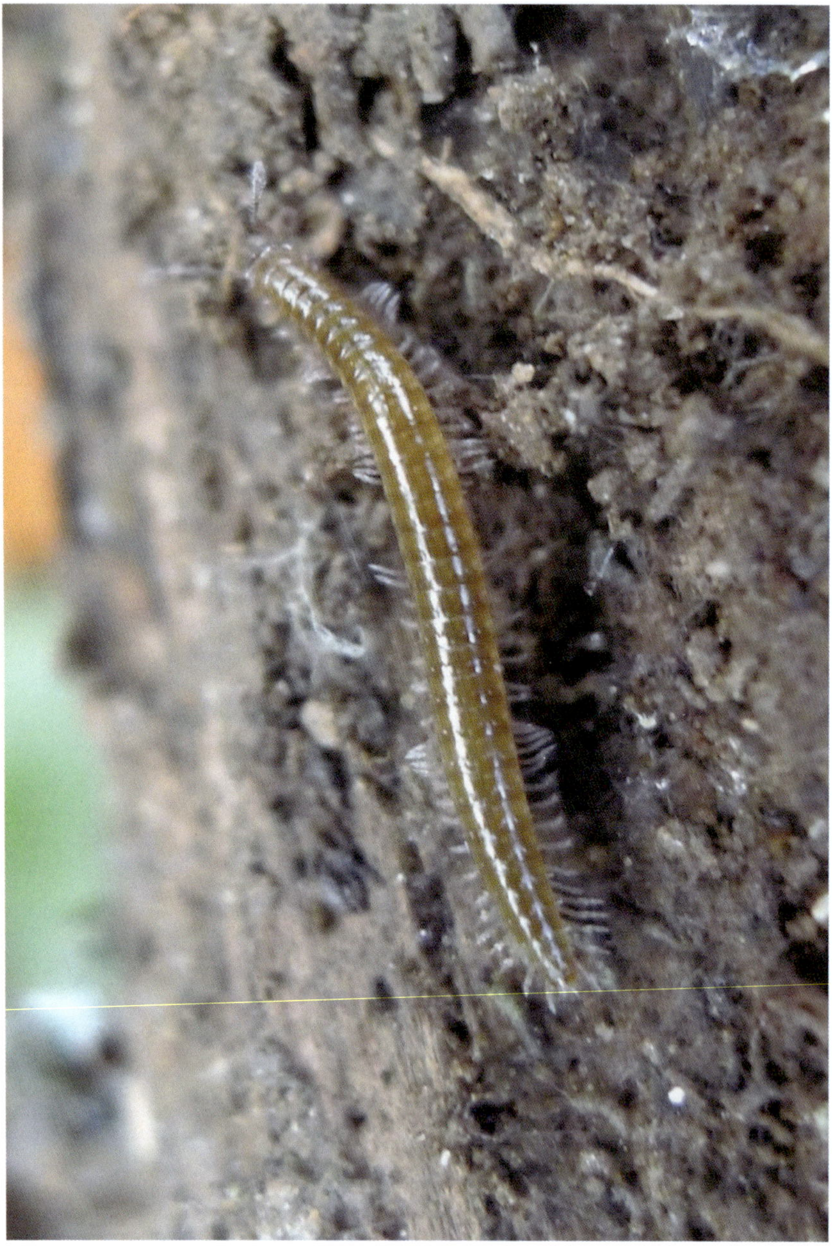

SUITABILITY AS PETS

Millipedes are often thought of as pests, but these small creatures can make great pets. Here are a few things to consider if you're thinking of adding a millipede to your home:

- First, they are generally very easy to care for. They don't require a lot of space or special equipment, and they can be fed a variety of common pet food items.

- Second, millipedes are low-maintenance pets that are unlikely to cause any problems in your home. They are not known to bite or sting, and they are not particularly messy.

- Finally, millipedes can be interesting and entertaining pets. Many people enjoy watching them and observing their behavior.

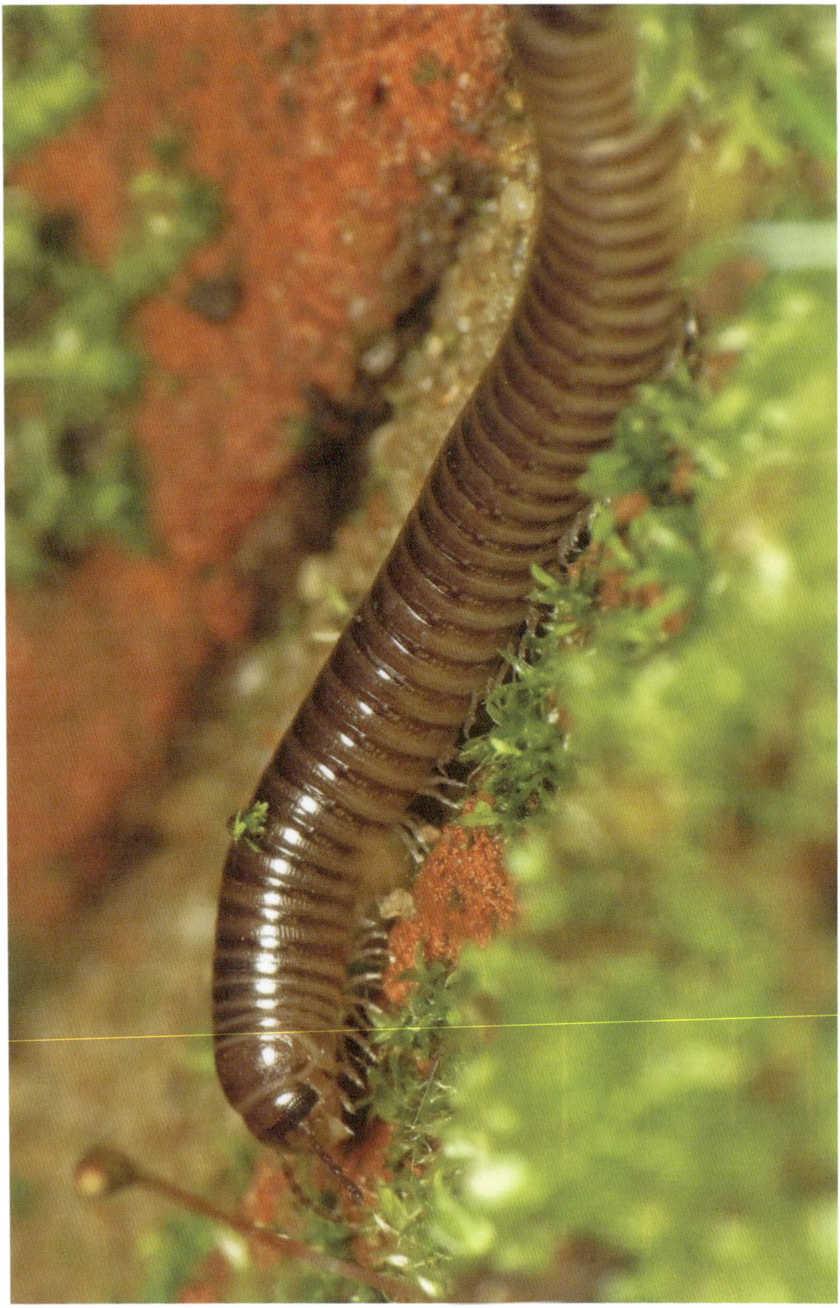

COLOR ME

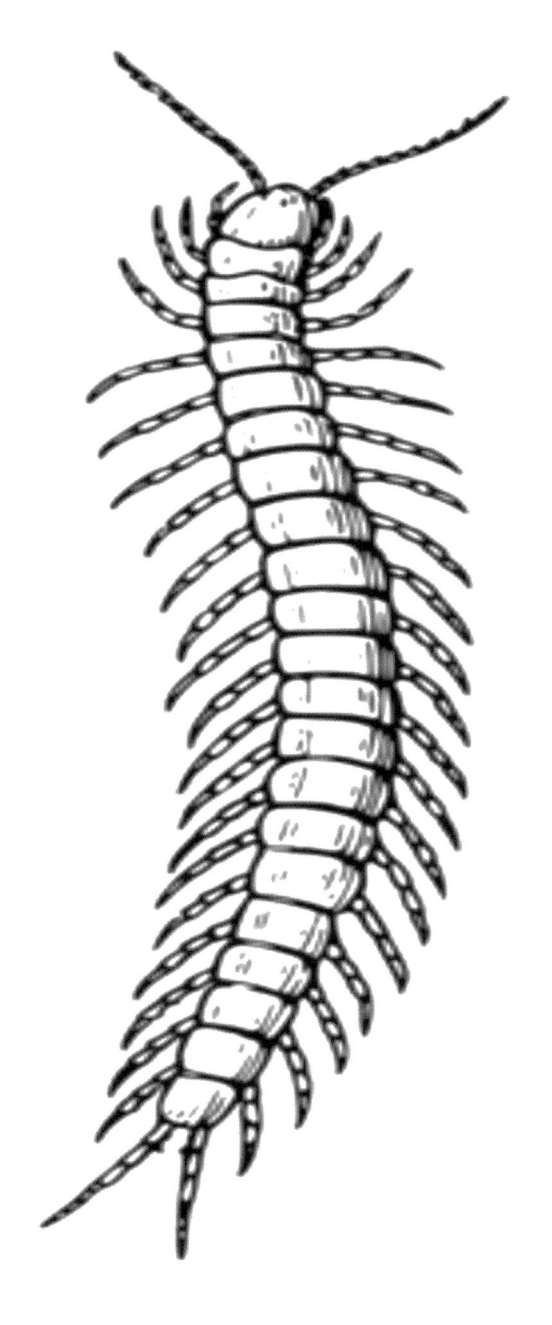

COLOR ME

COLOR ME

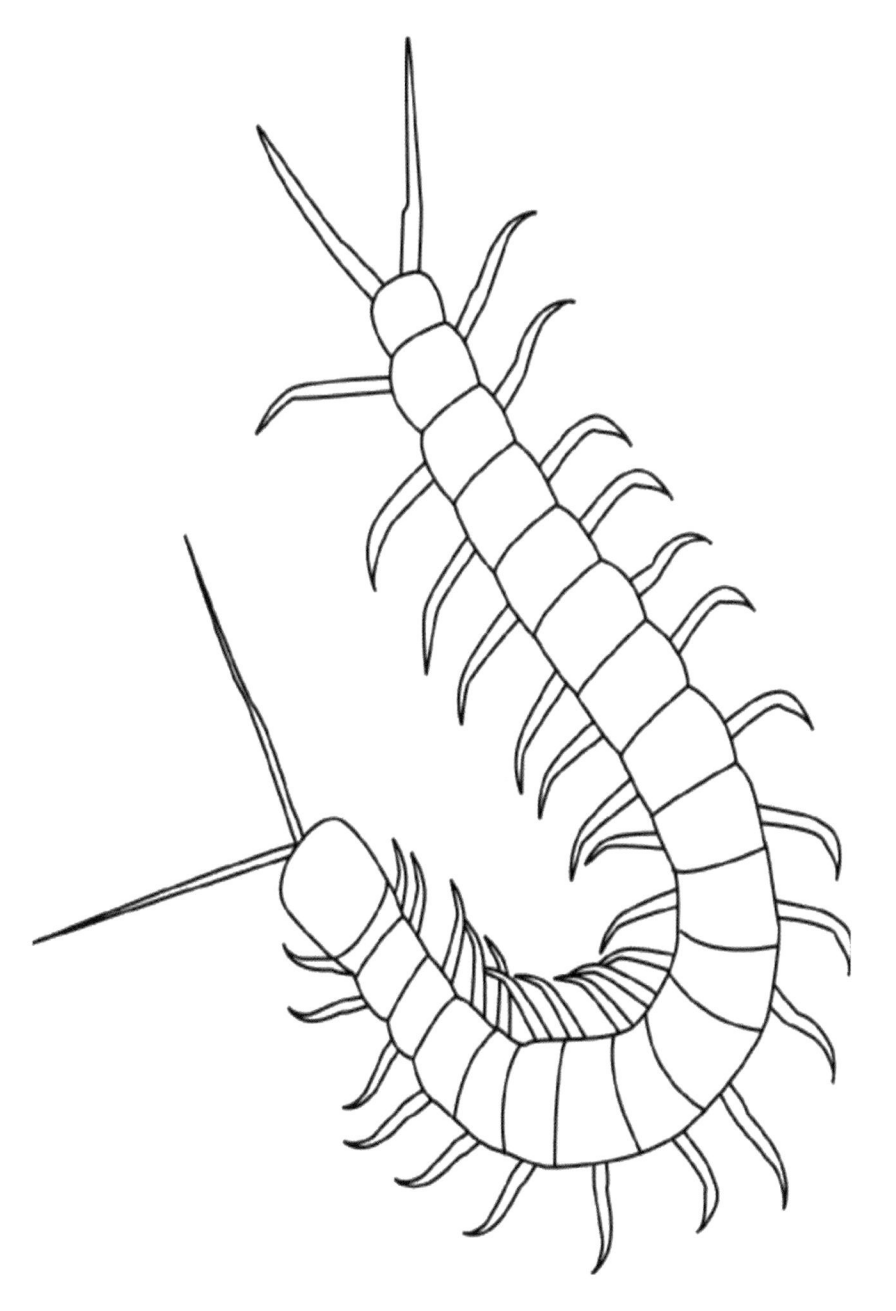

COLOR ME

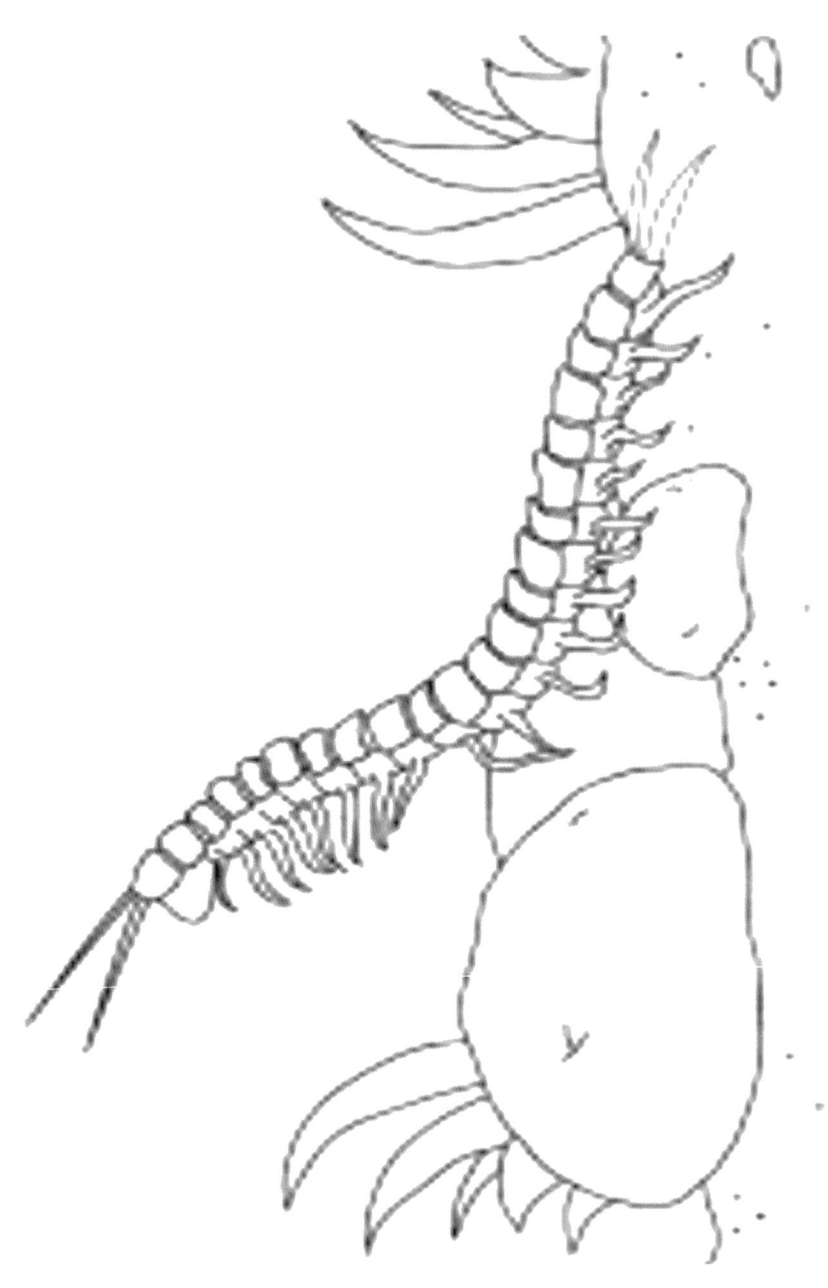

COLOR ME

COLOR ME

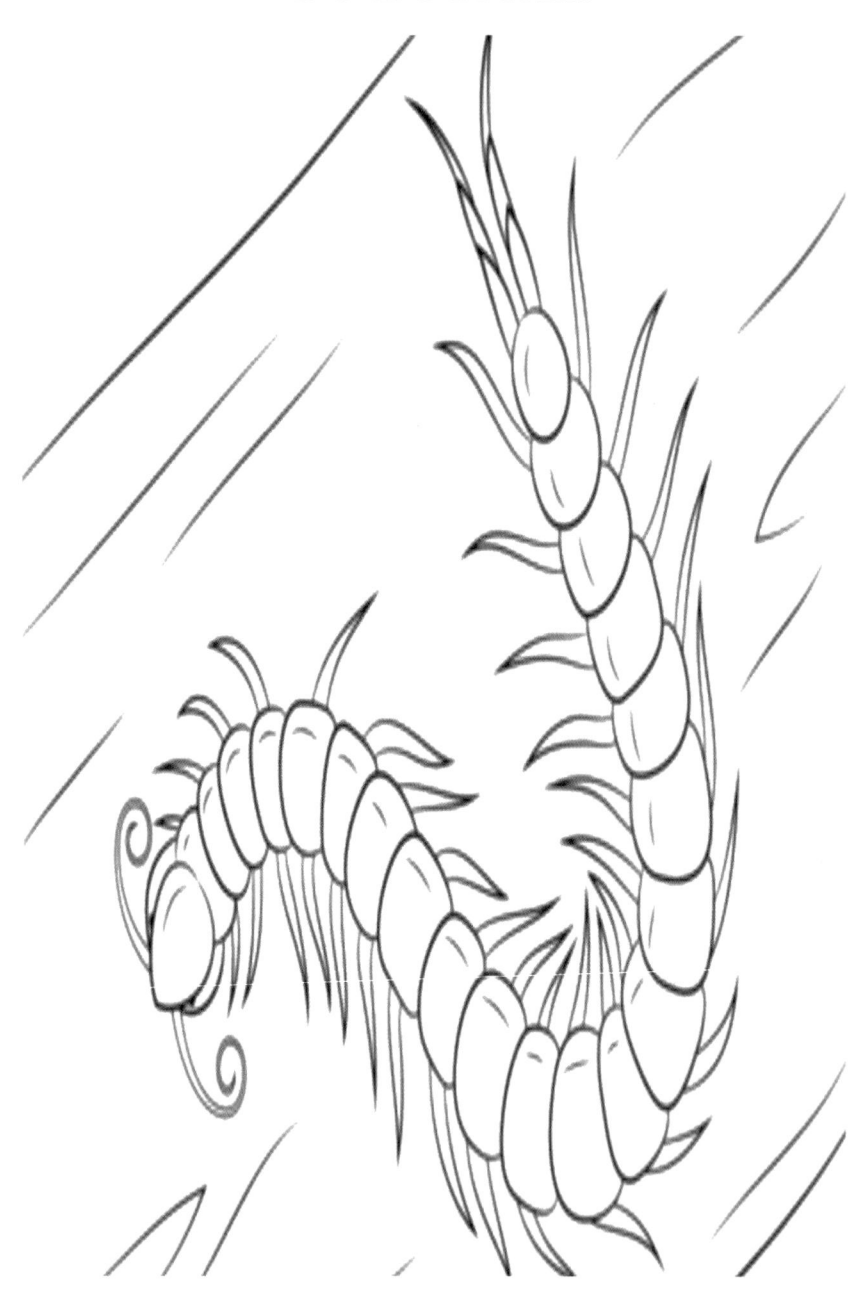

COLOR ME

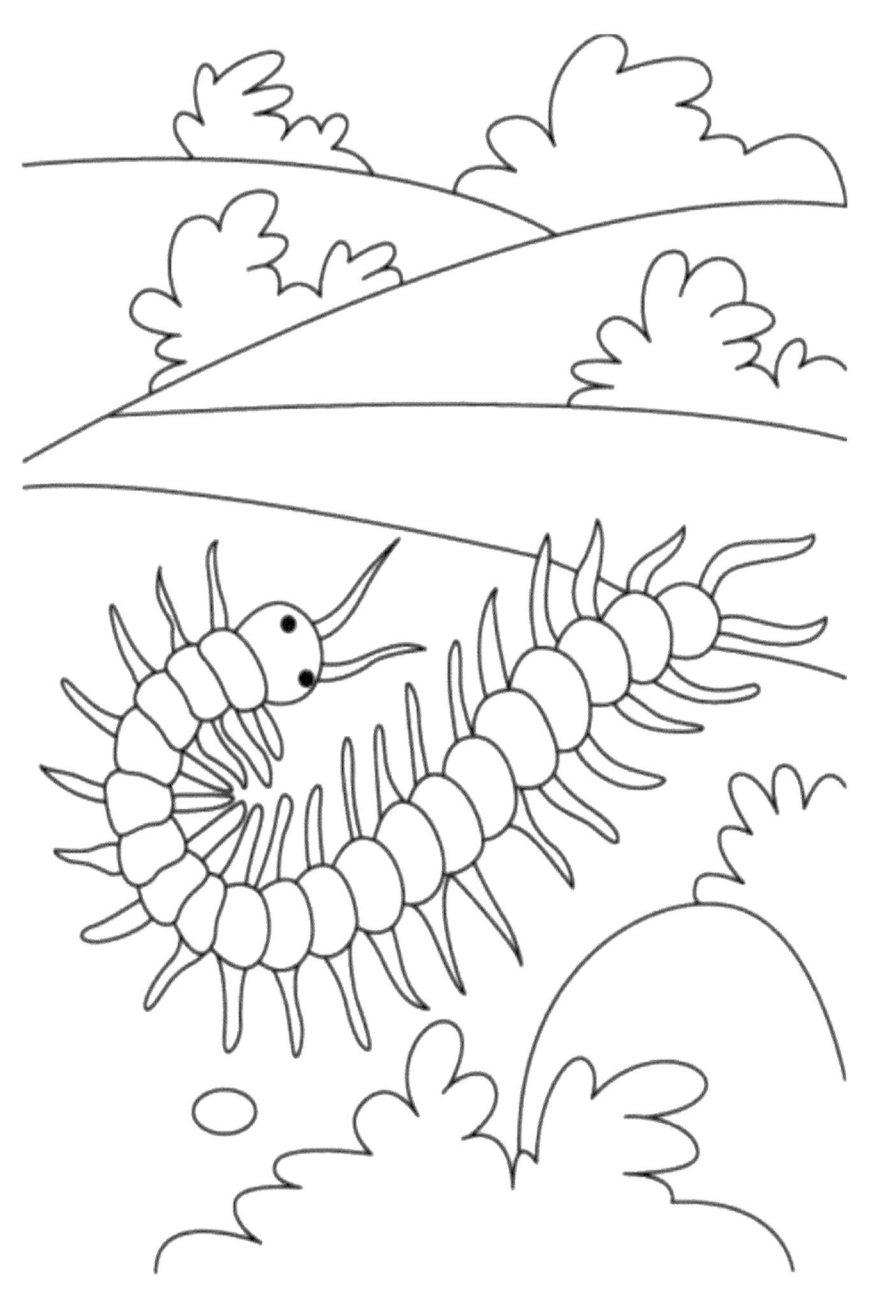

COLOR ME

COLOR ME

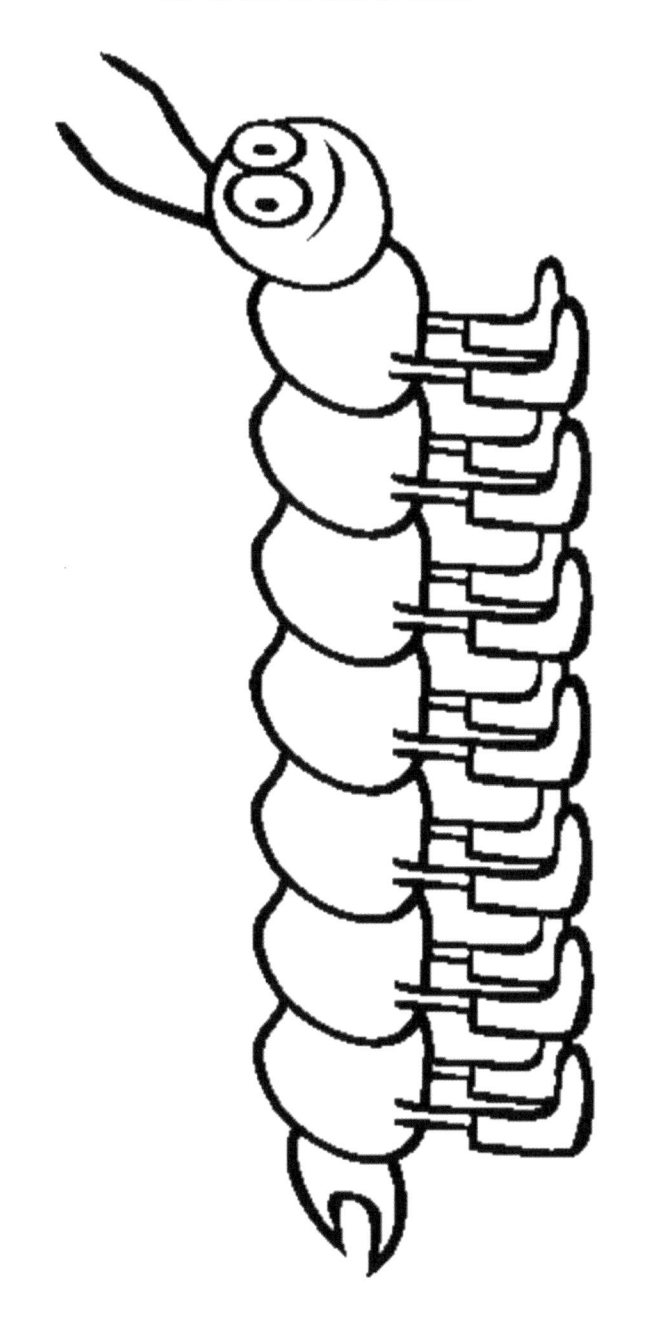

COLOR ME

Please leave me a review here:

LisaStrattin.com/Review-Vol-448

For more Kindle Downloads Visit Lisa Strattin Author Page on Amazon Author Central

amazon.com/author/lisastrattin

To see upcoming titles, visit my website at LisaStrattin.com– most books available on Kindle!

LisaStrattin.com

FREE BOOK

FOR ALL SUBSCRIBERS – SIGN UP NOW

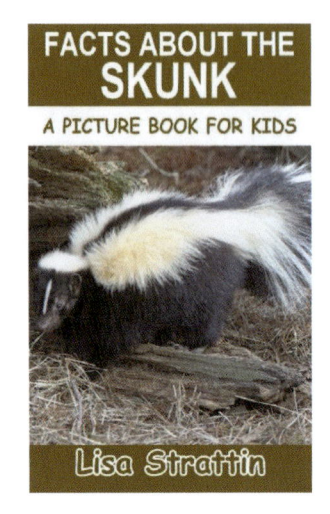

LisaStrattin.com/Subscribe-Here

LisaStrattin.com/Facebook

LisaStrattin.com/Youtube

Printed in Great Britain
by Amazon